342.0858 Mor
Morris, Neil
Do we have a right to
 privacy? #145431803 MAY 2 0 2008

What Do You Think?

Do We Have A Right To Privacy?

Neil Morris

Heinemann Library
Chicago, Illinois

©2008 Heinemann Library
a division of Reed Elsevier Inc.
100 N. LaSalle, Suite 1200, Chicago, Illinois

Customer Service 888-454-2279
Visit our website at www.heinemannraintree.com

All rights reserved. No part of this publication may be reproduced or transmitted in any form or by any means, electronic or mechanical, including photocopying, recording, taping, or any information storage and retrieval system, without permission in writing from the publisher.

Editorial: Andrew Farrow and Rebecca Vickers
Design: Steve Mead and Q2A Solutions
Picture Research: Melissa Allison
Production: Alison Parsons

Originated by Chroma Graphics Pte. Ltd.
Printed and bound in China by Leo Paper Group

12 11 10 09 08
10 9 8 7 6 5 4 3 2 1

ISBN: 978-1-4329-0354-1 (hardback)

Library of Congress Cataloging-in-Publication Data
Morris, Neil, 1946 –
  Do we have a right to privacy? / Neil Morris.
    p. cm. -- (What do you think?)
  Includes bibliographical references and index.
  ISBN-13: 978-1-4329-0354-1 (library binding – hardcover) 1.
  ISBN-10: 1-4329-0354-3 (library binding – hardcover) 1.
Privacy, right of--Juvenile literature. I. Title.
  K3263. M67 2008
  342. 08'58--dc22
                                                                    2007025956

Acknowledgments
The author and publishers are grateful to the following for permission to reproduce copyright material:

©Alamy pp. 51 (Frances Roberts), 49 (Rob Bartee); ©Corbis pp. 16 (Ed Kashi), 47 (epa/Pool/David Furst), 22 (Fabio Cardosa), 19 (Mike Simons), 7 (Najlah Feanny), 27 (Playboy Archive), 11 (Reuters), 43 (Reuters/Jagadeesh), 21 (Reuters/Jayanta Shaw), 39 (Reuters, Russell Boyce), 41 (San Francisco Chronicle/Liz Hafalla), 46 (zefa/Ausloeser), 25 (zefa/Joson); ©Getty Images pp. 28 (Scott Barbour), 12 (Taxi/Mason Morfit), 15, (The Image Bank/Lester Lefkowitz); ©istockphoto.com pp. 8, 24 (David H Lewis); ©Masterfile p. 4 (Brian Pieters); ©PA Photos p. 31 (West Midlands Police); ©Rex Features p. 37 (Master Photo Milano s.a.s.); ©Science Photo Library p. 33 (Volker Steger, Peter Arnold Inc.); ©TopFoto p. 44 (Topham Picturepoint 1999); ©WireImage p. 34 (Jean Baptiste Lacroix); ©www.CartoonStock.com p. 10.

Cover photo reproduced with permission of ©TIPS/Blend Images. Camera photo from ©Getty Images/PhotoDisc.

The publishers would like to thank Mary Kelly for her comments in the preparation of this title.

Every effort has been made to contact copyright holders of any material reproduced in this book. Any omissions will be rectified in subsequent printings if notice is given to the publisher.

Disclaimer
All the Internet addresses (URLs) given in this book were valid at the time of going to press. However, due to the dynamic nature of the Internet, some addresses may have changed, or sites may have changed or ceased to exist since publication. While the author and publishers regret any inconvenience this may cause readers, no responsibility for any such changes can be accepted by either the author or the publishers.

Table of Contents

What Do You Think?... 5
What Is Privacy?... 9
Can We Protect Identity And Security?................................. 13
Are We Always In Front Of The Camera?............................. 29
Do Celebrities Have Special Rights?....................................... 35
Is Big Brother Watching You?... 45
Find Out More 52
Glossary 54
Index 56

Some words are printed in bold, **like this**. You can find out what they mean in the glossary.

> *Talking things over*
> After sharing ideas and discussing opinions, it is easier to decide what *you* think about an issue.

What Do You Think?

The aim of this book is to encourage you to form your own opinion about the main question posed by its title: Do we have a right to privacy? You probably already have your own ideas, but perhaps some of the information and quotations from books and articles might persuade you to change your mind.

Most people have opinions about important issues. But rather than just having an opinion, it is much better to have an *informed* opinion about an issue. To be informed, you need to approach a subject with an open mind. You can consider the evidence for and against your opinion, and then figure out what you think is the best position on the issue. As far as privacy goes, there are lots of different aspects of the issue to take into consideration. Your overall answer to the big question—Do we have a right to privacy?—may well be "yes." But you might feel differently about certain aspects, such as the need for identity cards or the use of security cameras. This book presents many cases and lots of evidence, but it is not comprehensive. There are other things you might consider, including your own experience, the experiences of your friends and family, and information gained from reading other books, magazines, and newspapers.

Critical thinking

As you read this book and think about privacy issues, try to approach the topic using the tools of critical thinking. When we think critically, we set aside our own pre-formed views and ask questions about the information and ideas that are presented to us. This allows us to approach other people's ideas with an open and inquisitive mind. We might ask questions such as these:

- Is this information **biased**—in other words, does the writer have a reason or incentive to present the information in a certain way? Does the opinion based on the information favor one side unfairly without good reasons being given?
- Is the information credible (believable)? Is the point of view supported by good reasons and evidence? Does the evidence presented seem reliable?
- What assumptions does the writer make? Are facts taken for granted rather than investigated? Are the assumptions justified or not?
- Do the arguments rely on sound logic? Does the writer use good, sensible reasoning in his or her arguments and deductions?
- Does the writer state where the information comes from? Does it come from a reliable source?

There are many other questions you might ask of a particular statement. The point of critical thinking is to read texts with an open mind and a skeptical eye, aiming to form your own opinions after paying attention to other people's opinions and ideas.

Informed opinions

You probably already have opinions about your own privacy. You know what you think it is reasonable for others to know about you, for example. You would probably be shocked if someone read your diary or personal writings without your permission, or if you discovered that there was a secret camera hidden in your home or classroom. This book asks you to form opinions about broader issues related to privacy, including computer databanks, identity cards, the Internet, the use of security cameras, and the rights of celebrities.

When you form opinions about these different issues, try to make sure that you express them as arguments. An argument has three parts:

- Assertion: An assertion is a strong statement about your opinion.
- Reasoning: You should support your assertion with logical reasons.
- Evidence: Evidence supports your reasoning by providing facts or examples to show that your argument is valid.

> *Research tools*
> Libraries offer a wide range of opportunities to research facts and evidence. In addition to books and periodicals, there are Internet search engines to help you.

 Checklist for critical thinking

Critical thinkers . . .
✔ understand the difference between fact and opinion, and are able to distinguish facts from opinions in spoken and written language.
✔ assess the available evidence, evaluating it fairly and completely.
✔ acknowledge different perspectives on an issue, accepting that people may disagree about it and identifying the points of disagreement.
✔ identify assumptions and evaluate them for their validity and any bias.
✔ evaluate different points of view to inform their own opinion.
✔ support their own ideas with sound reasoning and evidence, taking into account conflicting ideas and facts.

> *The unwanted camera*

This person clearly does not want to be photographed. She probably feels that her personal space is being threatened. Also, she might not want others to know where she is or what she is doing. This can be a real problem for celebrities, who believe they have a right to a private life just like everyone else.

What Is Privacy?

Privacy refers to the condition of being free from being disturbed by other people. It includes not being observed or overheard by others, whether or not you know that other people can see or hear you. Many people try to keep their private and public lives separate. In both these aspects of their lives, people expect that certain things are kept private. For example, whether you are at home or at work, you would be shocked if you learned that a postal worker read your letters before delivering them.

You probably feel that you have a right to privacy in your own home, and certainly in your own room. In recent years, advances in technology have made people think even harder about their privacy. Most people use a computer at work, in school, or at home, and we all know that computers store information. So, it is possible that someone else might see what we have been writing or working on, just like a snooping postal worker with our letters. This book asks you to consider what you think is right and what you think we all have a right to. As far as rights and laws are concerned, it is not straightforward when it comes to privacy. That is because some people, such as some newspaper editors or police officers, might think that it is reasonable to find things out about others—for example, in cases where there is a possibility that someone may be harmed.

Human rights

International laws include the protection of a set of **human rights**. These are rights that most people believe belong to every person. They are based on the idea that every human being has worth and dignity, and that everyone deserves certain basic freedoms. Most of the international laws that protect human rights were developed and written by the **United Nations**, an organization that is dedicated to worldwide peace and security.

The right to be left alone

In December 1890 the *Harvard Law Review* published an article by Louis Brandeis and Samuel Warren called "The Right to Privacy." In it, the writers quoted a famous U.S. judge in defining privacy as "the right to be let alone" (we would probably say "left alone" today). Back then, they were already concerned about privacy issues that still bother us today. They wrote: "Instantaneous photographs and newspaper enterprise have invaded the sacred precincts of private and domestic life; and numerous mechanical devices threaten to make good the prediction that 'what is whispered in the closet shall be proclaimed from the house-tops.'"

"HE KNOWS IF YOU'VE BEEN BAD OR GOOD, BUT DON'T WORRY. PRIVACY RULES PREVENT HIM FROM DISCUSSING INDIVIDUAL CASES OR SITUATIONS."

> *Joking aside!*
> We can laugh about privacy rights, and humor can be used as part of the debate. But cartoons can make serious points, too.

> *Making a judgment*
The judges' president announces a verdict at the European Court of Human Rights in Strasbourg, France. The court hears many cases concerning privacy rights.

Universal Declaration of Human Rights

In December 1948 the General Assembly of the United Nations adopted the Universal Declaration of Human Rights. Though this was a set of aims rather than laws, the UN asked all member countries to publicize the declaration. Article 12 reads: "No one shall be subjected to arbitrary interference with his privacy, family, home or correspondence, nor to attacks upon his honor and reputation. Everyone has the right to the protection of the law against such interference or attacks."

The European Convention on Human Rights

The Council of Europe is an organization with members from over 40 European countries. It is dedicated to protecting issues such as human rights. In November 1950 the Council of Europe published its own declaration on human rights, including Article 8:

1. Everyone has the right to respect for his private and family life, his home, and his correspondence.

2. There shall be no interference by a public authority with the exercise of this right except such as is in accordance with the law and is necessary in a democratic society in the interests of national security, public safety, or the economic well-being of the country, for the prevention of disorder or crime, for the protection of health or morals, or for the protection of the rights and freedoms of others.

> *Modern databanks*

Today, most large companies have huge databanks.
Many contain personal information about customers.

Can We Protect Identity And Security?

How do you feel about databanks? It probably depends on what information they contain and what they are used for. You may use a library database regularly, and it would seem strange if you could not look up authors as well as individual books. But you would not expect the database to give you any personal information about an author (such as a phone number), and you would not want it to demand private details from you before you used it.

There are laws to limit the way in which databases disclose information. Most require the use of user names and passwords to gain access. Still, hackers manage to break into them.

People have strong feelings about databanks and privacy. Identity cards are a good example (see page 20). Some people think that ID cards could help fight crime and are therefore a good thing. If you have nothing to hide, they say, why worry? But others say there are at least two good reasons why ID cards are a concern. First, the state authorities can use information about you in ways that you might not be aware of or want. Second, hackers could find personal information about you and perhaps even steal your identity.

Debating databanks

People might be frightened of the misuse of databanks, but they also realize that databanks can be very useful. We are used to looking up numbers in a phone book, but most of us probably agree it is a good idea not to be forced to list our own number in the book. If you have a cell phone, you probably have your own small databank stored in its memory. But you might not want others to get hold of the list—for the sake of your own privacy and that of your friends.

Is security a joke?

Many databanks are privately owned by commercial firms. They act as any private company does by selling their products—in this case, personal information about millions of people.

In 2005 the U.S. Senate Committee on the Judiciary held a hearing on how to secure electronic personal data. One of those asked to testify was Robert Douglas, chief executive of PrivacyToday.com. Here is some of what he said:

> "Information security in the U.S. is laughable at best. But even if all legitimate information brokers were to appropriately and effectively secure the data in their electronic warehouses, the flow of information would continue. Criminals and others will just access, and in many cases continue to access, databases from the government and private sector to find the personal information they need for their crimes.
>
> "When it comes to the overwhelming majority of databases in this country, from government maintained military, postal, education, tax, welfare, and child support records, to commercially maintained financial accounts, telecommunications, utility, medical, and business records, the information can almost always be obtained by an individual named in the records. . . . For the unscrupulous information broker or criminal, it is merely a matter of piecing together enough personal information about the targeted victim to impersonate the victim to the custodian of the information."

Deadly data

So, how do we find the balance? There is a legitimate need for records to be kept, but is it possible to guarantee the accuracy and security of the records? With so much information already out there, making sure that only those with a real need can access the data has become increasingly difficult . . . and even deadly. In 1989 an obsessed fan-turned-stalker was able to obtain actress Rebecca Shaeffer's address from the California Department of Motor Vehicles. He then went to her home and shot the young actress dead. This source is no longer available to the public, but in the nearly 20 years since Shaeffer's death, the number of databases with the same type of information has exploded.

> *In the olden days*
Filing cabinets full of folders and files seem very old-fashioned now. They cannot hold nearly as much data as modern computers and take up a lot more space.

The war on terror

The phrase "war on terror" (or "war on terrorism") was introduced by the U.S. government following the attacks on the World Trade Center in New York City and the Pentagon, near Washington, D.C., on September 11, 2001 (9/11). Since then the phrase has been linked to the question of privacy rights because the U.S. government brought in new laws to fight terrorism. These allow law-enforcement officers to intercept communications to and from terrorist suspects.

The USA PATRIOT Act

The USA PATRIOT Act was passed in October 2001, a month after the 9/11 attacks. The name of the act is a clever **acronym**. USA PATRIOT stands for **U**niting and **S**trengthening **A**merica by **P**roviding **A**ppropriate **T**ools **R**equired to **I**ntercept and **O**bstruct **T**errorism. Of course, the word "patriot" also means a person who strongly and proudly supports his or her country.

Among other powers, the PATRIOT Act allows officials greater freedom to conduct a search of somebody's home, in some cases without even telling that person. It also widens the power of the authorities to use **wiretapping**—a device that can monitor a phone line, email, voice mail, or Internet activity. Some people say that wiretapping is a major threat to people's privacy, and that it goes against the wording of the Universal Declaration of Human Rights (see page 11). The law also gives the authorities more freedom to access information banks and medical records.

> *Office of Emergency Management*
> At this office in Chicago, operatives use video camera images to keep a lookout for criminal activity. They can quickly send officers to investigate.

Making the case for the act

This is an extract from the statement of President George W. Bush in March 2006, on the passing of the bill to reauthorize the USA PATRIOT Act:

> "I applaud the Senate for voting to renew the Patriot Act. . . . The terrorists have not lost the will or the ability to attack us. The Patriot Act is vital to the war on terror and defending our **citizens** against a ruthless enemy. This bill will allow our law-enforcement officials to continue to use the same tools against terrorists that are already used against drug dealers and other criminals, while safeguarding the **civil liberties** of the American people."

In his statement on the bill, U.S. Attorney General Alberto R. Gonzales supported the president's view:

> "Since the terrible attacks of September 11, 2001, the Department of Justice's highest priority has been to protect Americans by preventing acts of terrorism. . . . Importantly the legislation provides additional tools for protecting our mass transport systems and seaports from attack; takes steps to combat the methamphetamine epidemic that is sweeping our country; and closes dangerous loopholes in our ability to prevent terrorist financing."

The case against the act

Amnesty International, an organization that undertakes research and action focused on promoting all human rights, has a different view about the act:

> "Amnesty International is concerned that the USA PATRIOT Act undermines the human rights of Americans and **non-citizens,** and weakens the framework for promoting human rights internationally.
>
> "Amnesty International is concerned that the USA PATRIOT Act infringes on the right to privacy and removes many types of **judicial review** over

(continued on page 18)

intelligence activities. [The act] permits the government to scrutinize people's reading habits by monitoring public library and bookstore records, without notifying the suspect. It also allows for 'sneak and peak' tactics such as physical search of property and computers, wiretapping and monitoring of email, and access to financial and educational records, without providing notification. . . . The 'war on terror' must not be an excuse to deny human rights. September 11, 2001, caused many to reflect upon the fundamental values on which this country was founded: freedom of speech, respect for human dignity, freedom of religion, justice for all, tolerance. It is **imperative** that the United States stand for the principles of unalienable, universal rights. Otherwise, those who wage war on human rights will have won the battle against freedom. Amnesty International is concerned the 'war on terror' not become an excuse to deny human rights."

What other people think

Here is a Gallup Poll on what people think about the act. It is interesting because it suggests that, over time, some people began to worry more about civil liberties. People were asked: "Based on what you have read or heard, do you think the Patriot Act goes too far, is about right, or does not go far enough in restricting people's civil liberties in order to fight terrorism?"

The USA PATRIOT Act Gallup Poll results

	Too far	*About right*	*Not far enough*	*No opinion*
Jan. 2006	38 %	40 %	19 %	3 %
Feb. 2004	26 %	43 %	21 %	10 %
Aug. 2003	22 %	48 %	21 %	9 %

> *Supporting the USA PATRIOT Act*

Then-Attorney General John Ashcroft defends the act in front of an audience of law-enforcement officers in September 2003. One of the act's slogans, "Preserving Life and Liberty," is on the podium web address.

 Comparing and contrasting views

Do these views about the USA PATRIOT Act convince you either way? Are they credible? Biased? Based on sound logic? When evaluating the viewpoints, look carefully at the terms used on both sides. Some are quite emotive, which means they are intended to arouse intense emotional feelings in the reader. On one side there are words and phrases such as "vital," "ruthless enemy," and "dangerous loopholes." These people make the argument: What is more important, our right to privacy (and civil liberty), or freedom from terrorist attacks?

On the other side, terms such as "undermine" (meaning "damage" or "weaken") and "sneak and peak" are used. You might think some of these terms, on both sides, show bias. Or you could take the view that they show how strongly the people feel about the issue. The other thing you need to consider is whether there is evidence to support their claims.

A question of terminology

Do you think the term "war on terror" is a good one? Do you think it influences people? A report in *The Observer* newspaper stated that in Great Britain, politicians have been told to stop using the term because it may "anger British Muslims and increase tensions more broadly in the Islamic world." However, a spokesperson for the U.S. State Department said that "there was no question of dropping the term." "It's the president's phrase, and that's good enough for us," she said.

Identity cards and privacy

There has been a lot of talk in the newspapers and on television about identity cards. Some countries—such as the United States—do not have official ID cards at all. But other countries—such as Germany and Spain—have compulsory ID cards. Australia, France, and other countries have non-compulsory cards. Many people are worried about ID cards because they feel that they represent an invasion of their privacy. They are also concerned that the card's details might fall into the wrong hands.

The privacy implications of ID cards

The organization Privacy International gives a lot of thought to ID cards. The organization calls itself "a human rights group formed as a watchdog on surveillance and privacy invasions by governments and corporations." The text below reflects how it answers the question, "What are the privacy implications of an ID card?"

```
"In short, the implications are profound. The existence
of a person's life story in a hundred unrelated databases
is one important condition that protects privacy. The
bringing together of these separate information centers
creates a major privacy vulnerability. Any multi-purpose
national ID card has this effect.

"Some privacy advocates . . . argue against ID cards on
the basis of evidence from various security threat models
in use throughout the private sector. In these models,
it is generally assumed that at any one time, 1 percent
of staff will be willing to sell or trade confidential
information for personal gain. In many European
countries, up to 1 percent of bank staff are dismissed
each year, often because of theft.

"The evidence for this potential corruption is
compelling. Recent inquiries in Australia, Canada, and
the United States indicate that widespread abuse of
computerized information is occurring."
```

Do you think this argument against ID cards is well made? Is there really evidence of "potential corruption"—in other words "possible crime"? Perhaps there is an assumption that a certain small number of people (1 percent) will always try to steal from others? Also, doesn't "up to 1 percent" really mean "less than 1 percent"?

> *Identifying the right to vote*
> These women in India line up to show the identity cards that confirm their right to vote in a national election. Do you think this system is a good idea?

What about other forms of ID?

In many countries, passports and driver licences are used instead of official ID cards. In the United States, the Social Security card and its number are also used. Some people are very worried about this, as shown in this article.

```
Who's Got Your Number?
The quickest way to become a victim of identity theft
is to let your Social Security number (SSN) fall into
the wrong hands. That's why a group of employees are
suing Union Pacific Railroad over the casual way the
company used the numbers to ID workers—a practice that
became a real issue in April when a computer with the
names and numbers of 30,000 employees was stolen. In May
someone made off with a laptop containing the SSNs of
26.5 million people on file at the Department of Veterans
Affairs—which suggests that it's more important than ever
to keep your number under wraps. A lot of groups ask for
it; very few really need it. Just be ready for a fight.

[Source: Barbara Kiviat, Time magazine, July 2006]
```

Identity theft

Like many others, the *Time* writer quoted on page 21 is worried about identity theft. The founder of an organization called Privacy Rights Clearinghouse has contributed to the World Book encyclopedia entry on this worrying crime:

> Identity theft is the use of another individual's personal information—such as name, Social Security number, driver's license number, or credit card number—to commit fraud. Identity thieves may obtain private information by stealing wallets, sifting through trash, stealing mail, or breaking into computer systems. They may then use the stolen information to pose as another person while accessing bank and credit card accounts, purchasing goods and services, or engaging in illegal activity.

Would you agree that the encyclopedia entry is unbiased? The writer uses clear language to define the term "identity theft." There are no emotive adjectives.

> *Patient data*
> Computer records are helpful to doctors, but are they a privacy worry for patients?

Medical records

Most people are sensitive about their medical history. Many governments are in the process of creating central databanks full of patients' details. Those who are in favor of this system say it will help doctors and patients. Opponents worry that the information will not remain private and confidential.

In the United States, under the Department of Health and Human Services, plans are well underway for the development of a national electronic health record (EHR) system. When in place (sometime in the next 10 years), this system will be able to share clinical data online across the health care industry. For example, if someone from Florida becomes sick or is involved in an accident in California, the EHR system allows the doctor treating that individual to access medical records, including test results, previous treatment, and current medication use.

But does this kind of system raise privacy and security issues? The more people who can access records, surely the less secure they become. Also, if there are errors in the records, what happens when those errors become available to a wider audience? An article in the *Guardian* newspaper (November 2, 2006) highlighted the case of a woman in England who found out that her incorrect medical records were out of her control:

```
Helen Wilkinson was mistakenly labeled an alcoholic
after a simple computer error by the NHS [Britain's
National Health Service]. An unknown official at a
hospital was updating her medical records and inputted
a wrong code. The mix-up meant she was recorded as
having received treatment for alcoholism, instead of
surgery. Ms Wilkinson, 40, was furious and began a
campaign to have all information about her permanently
removed from the hospital's databanks. But she ran
into a problem: the NHS already keeps electronic
records on everyone who receives treatment from the
health service, whether they are seen by a GP [General
Practitioner; a doctor] or at a hospital.
```

Internet issues

Computer experts say that Internet privacy does not really exist. Yet most people would probably say that when they surf the Web, they should be completely anonymous and their surfing should be private. Are you concerned about this? How much Internet privacy do you think people should be allowed? As the use of the Internet continues to grow—at home, in schools, and in businesses— these questions will become more and more important.

> *Work and the Web*
>
> When an employee goes on to a website, the employer's Internet domain name is usually collected and stored by the website. The employer might also keep a record of the sites accessed by the employee.

What happens when you surf?

When you visit Internet websites, they usually automatically collect and store your Internet domain (for example, "my-company.com" or "my-school.edu") and Internet protocol (IP) address. The IP is a number that is automatically assigned to your computer whenever you surf the Web. Websites might also know the type of browser and operating system you use, the date and time you access any site, and the individual pages you visit.

Beyond that, websites will know only what you decide to tell them. You might give your email address, for example, or even more details if you want to be able to log on to special offers. But, in this case, at least you know what information you are giving out. Is this how we want our privacy to work?

Privacy policies

All large websites have a privacy policy, and if you click on the link in the small print at the bottom of the site's home page, you can read what they say they do and do not do. On page 25, there is an example from the White House site, www.whitehouse.gov.

White House Website Privacy and Security Policy
"We will collect no personal information about you when you visit our website unless you choose to provide that information to us. . . . If you do nothing during your visit but browse through the website, read pages, or download information, we will gather and store certain information about your visit automatically. This information does not identify you personally. We use this information to help us make our site more useful to visitors—to learn about the number of visitors to our site and the types of technology our visitors use. We do not track or record information about individuals and their visits. The information you provide is not given to any private organizations or private persons. The White House does not collect or use information for commercial marketing."

> *Laptop privacy*

People all over the world, such as this businessman in Vietnam, find laptop computers useful. But think of all the private information they hold and expose to hackers.

Cookies

Cookies are small text files that are placed on a user's computer and allow websites to remember information about that user. When you return to a website, the existing cookie allows it to personalize information and save you time. For example, if you have registered with a company, the cookie will help it recognize who you are and offer you your own account. If you want to, you can delete cookies from your browser.

Leaking information

On August 4, 2006, the media company and Internet service provider AOL released a text file on one of its websites containing 20 million search keywords. They had been keyed in by more than 650,000 users over a three-month period and were intended for research purposes. After complaints, AOL removed the file three days later. Although the searchers were only identified by a number ID, the *New York Times* managed to discover the identity of several of them. With her permission, it revealed number 4417749 to be Thelma Arnold, a 62-year-old widow from Georgia. This breach of privacy was widely reported and led to the resignation of AOL's chief technical officer.

Email

You can never be certain that emails will remain private. In most countries the privacy laws on correspondence (which originally covered the postal service) cover email. That means it is illegal to eavesdrop on other people's electronic correspondence. But it does not stop hackers and con artists from doing it.

To make this difficult, Internet service providers should encrypt e-messages. That means turning information into a secret code, so that the receiving ISP has to decrypt the code, turning it back into readable language. Sensitive information, such as credit card numbers given to online sellers, has to be securely encrypted.

Snooping Bosses

```
Think your employer is checking your email, Web searches,
and voice mail? You're probably right.
```

```
When one of his employees phoned in sick last
year, Scott McDonald, CEO of Monument Security in
Sacramento, Calif., decided to investigate. He had
```

already informed his staff of 400 security guards and patrol drivers that he was installing Xora, a software program that tracks workers' whereabouts through GPS technology on their company cell phones. A Web-based "geo-fence" around work territories would alert the boss if workers strayed or even drove too fast. It also enabled him to route workers more efficiently. So when McDonald logged on, the program told him exactly where his worker was—and it wasn't in bed with the sniffles. "How come you're eastbound on 80 heading to Reno right now if you're sick?" asked the boss. There was a long silence—the sound of a job ending—followed by, "You got me."

[Source: Kristina Dell, Lisa Takeuchi Cullen, *Time* magazine, September 3, 2006]

In the United States and some other countries, email messages sent by company computers are considered company property and can be read by management. Employees should be told that they have no expectation of a right to privacy for messages sent or received on company equipment. Do you think that is right? Should employers be allowed to invade their employees' privacy, even if it turns out they were right to suspect them of cheating the company? What do you think about the following example?

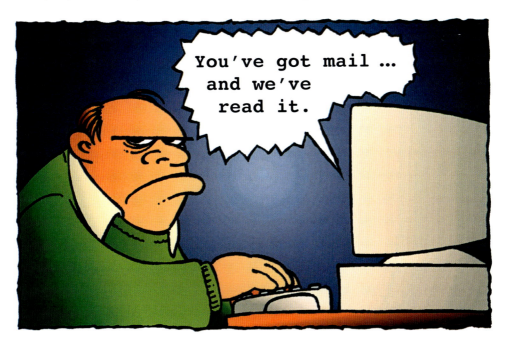

> *Email security*
Emails are hard to keep private or to delete permanently.

> *Are you being watched?*
> Security cameras, like this one, are usually quite small and sometimes difficult to spot.

Are We Always In Front Of The Camera?

You have probably noticed that there are more security cameras around than there used to be. They work by a system called closed-circuit television (**CCTV**). The cameras transmit pictures by cable to a limited number of connected monitors. These form a "closed circuit," and the pictures are not broadcast via antennas or satellite dishes. The first CCTV system was used in Germany in 1942 to observe the test launch of military rockets. CCTV is still useful in industry, as it allows researchers to watch processes that they cannot see easily themselves.

But today, CCTV is mostly used for surveillance, because it can provide continual observation of a particular location. Operatives can watch live pictures, which are recorded on video so that they can be reviewed at a later time. The use of CCTVs in the United States has increased massively since the terrorist attacks on September 11, 2001. In 1998 New York's Times Square had 75 CCTVs. There are now over 600 in the same area. The use of security cameras is more common in Europe.

Crime detection

CCTV cameras are mostly used to prevent crime and to catch criminals. The idea is that people will see the cameras, or signs pointing out that video surveillance is in operation, and make sure that they behave well. If they do commit a crime, they must realize that they will be caught on camera, recognized, and brought to justice. A website that puts people in contact with companies selling CCTV systems puts it this way:

```
"Statistics point to major reductions in the amount of
crime being committed where there are cameras installed.
An article in New Scientist magazine showed that simply
installing a system can reduce crime, in the areas
covered, by over 95 percent. As our customers inform us
that they are having similar results in all types of
business, you will begin to appreciate why CCTV is seen by
many as the best system for deterrent and detection. . . .

"Generally, once a Camera system is installed, it will
only be fools who attempt to perpetrate offenses within
its field of view. These are often caught but for the
majority it will provide a very high level of deterrence."
```

Certainly there have been major successes in finding criminals. For example, surveillance cameras in the United Kingdom helped to identify the suicide bombers who were responsible for four explosions in London on July 7, 2005. The police watched thousands of hours of CCTV video taken near railroad stations. They found pictures of four men carrying large backpacks arriving at a station in London.

What do they think?

"CCTV doesn't bother me in my day-to-day life. It's only when asked that I feel a tinge of resentment at the atmosphere of distrust they create. But I have no problem ignoring them for the sake of their law enforcement and regular protection."
Bella, 18, student

"As a law-abiding citizen, I have nothing to hide and so have no problem with public surveillance systems. If smart CCTV helps prevent and solve crimes in any way, then it has my full backing."
Will, 27, TV producer

> *Caught on camera*
The police released this surveillance-camera photo of a man who threatened to rob a fast-food restaurant.

Doubting the evidence

Some people doubt the evidence regarding CCTV. They believe that security cameras are an invasion of people's privacy. According to Privacy International:

```
"The extent of concern was highlighted by the outcome
that more than 50 percent of people felt neither
government nor private security firms should be allowed
to make decisions to allow the installation of CCTV
in public places. Seventy-two percent agreed 'these
cameras could easily be abused and used by the wrong
people.' Thirty-nine percent felt that people who are
in control of these systems could not be 'completely
trusted to use them only for the public good.' Thirty-
seven percent felt that 'in the future, cameras will
be used by the government to control people.' While
this response could be interpreted a number of ways,
it goes to the heart of the privacy and civil rights
dilemma. More than one respondent in ten believed that
CCTV cameras should be banned."
```

What do you think? Do the benefits outweigh the downside?

Smart systems

New "smart" systems include face-recognition devices that can scan video images to identify people already stored in a computer databank. There was a famous use of this system at the 2001 Super Bowl, which is described below.

Uncle Sam and the Watching Eye

Over the past few months there had been a growing backlash in America against the installation of "smart" closed-circuit television (CCTV) systems in public places. In January, a smart CCTV system was used to scan the faces of the 72,000 people going to watch the Super Bowl in Tampa, Florida, as they passed through the turnstiles of the Raymond James Stadium. Their faces were covertly compared with a database of known criminals, using a facial-recognition system. When details of the operation emerged, it was condemned by civil-liberties groups, who called it "snooper bowl."

The recent installation of a similar system to scan the faces of pedestrians in Ybor City, Tampa's entertainment district, has been denounced as "digital frisking" that makes pedestrians take part in a "virtual police line-up." Over the summer, newspaper columnists repeated the message: unless Americans took a stand, their country would soon come to resemble Europe, where use of CCTV is far more prevalent. . . . As in Tampa, such systems are routinely justified on anti-terrorism grounds, and encounter little opposition in places such as Britain and Spain, whose citizens are used to living with the threat of terrorism.

[Source: *The Economist* newspaper, September 22, 2001]

Biometrics

Smart CCTV systems use an identification method called **biometrics**. Computers scan images to recognize certain physical characteristics, such as fingerprints, voices, or facial structure. A biometric system can operate in one of two ways. The first is that of true identification, determining who an individual is out of a large population. For example, a system might be used to identify someone crossing a border by photographing the person's face.

It then compares the information with stored images to find a match. This was the system used at the Super Bowl game.

More commonly, biometrics is simply used to verify that people are who they claim to be. The personal identification numbers (PINs) that people use to gain access to banking systems are an example of a verification device. With a biometric system, the PIN would be replaced by a scan of a physical trait.

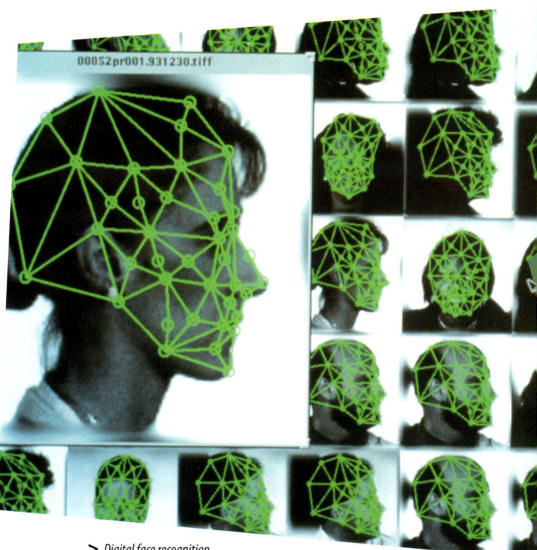

> *Digital face recognition*
> This biometric system is based on facial structure and especially the distance and direction between certain points on a person's head. In addition to face recognition, the unique qualities of every eye's iris means the iris can also be used for individual recognition.

> *In the public eye*

Celebrities, such as movie star Charlize Theron, shown here at the Cannes Film Festival, are used to being photographed wherever they go.

Do Celebrities Have Special Rights?

Most people would probably agree that "freedom of the press" is important. It gives all the media—newspapers, magazines, book publishers, and TV and radio networks—the right to publish facts, opinions, and photographs without interference or **censorship**. But most people are not celebrities, and many of our favorite movie stars, athletes, and TV personalities might have a very different view. That is because the media are very often interested in the private lives of public figures. Most countries have laws against invasion of privacy, but invasive journalism is difficult to define. It depends on individual cases, so many celebrity disputes end up going to court for a judge and jury to decide.

The press's defense against a charge of invasion of privacy is usually that the words or pictures in question are "in the public interest." This certainly applies to the kind of investigative journalism that looks into shady dealings by business people or politicians. But are details of a movie star's vacation on a Caribbean island "in the public interest"?

Interest versus intrusion

One person's interest (for example, that of a journalist and a newspaper reader) is another person's intrusion (that felt by the famous subject of the journalist's article). Those of us who are not famous do not have to worry—the media will probably never focus on us, because their audience will not show the necessary interest. But celebrities have to put up with the press, especially the **paparazzi** photographers who look for any opportunity to take pictures of them.

Snapping celebrities

A paparazzo is a freelance photographer who specializes in pursuing celebrities to take pictures of them. The word comes from the name of a character in the 1960 movie *La Dolce Vita*. In the movie, Paparazzo is an aggressive, scandal-seeking news photographer. Today's real-life paparazzi use hi-tech digital cameras with telephoto lenses. This means they can get close-ups that can be very quickly distributed and printed in newspapers and magazines. The paparazzi make it their business to know where celebrities are to be found. This means using contacts to find out where a movie star might be having lunch, which gym a supermodel uses to work out, or where a famous athlete is vacationing.

Battling the paparazzi

In recent years, celebrities have increasingly found their safety threatened by paparazzi eager for a picture (see opposite). In light of such problems, in 1998 the state of California, where many celebrities live, passed the Anti-Paparazzi Act. This creates penalties when a person trespasses "in order to physically invade the privacy of the plaintiff with the intent to capture any type of visual image, sound recording, or other physical impression of the plaintiff engaging in a personal or familial activity and the physical invasion occurs in a manner that is offensive to a reasonable person." Even without trespassing, the photographer is liable if the celebrity is "engaging in a personal or familial activity under circumstances in which the plaintiff had a reasonable expectation of privacy." In January 2006 the act was amended so that celebrities can now sue for any damages resulting from an aggressive encounter with the paparazzi. If the celebrity wins the suit, the photographer must pay up to three times the cost of the damages. Moreover, the photographer cannot make any profit from the photographs or video obtained.

Do you think this is fair? Or does it violate the freedom of the press?

Lindsay Calls in the Law

Despite transforming herself from a voluptuous redhead into a skinny blond, Lindsay Lohan still can't blend into Los Angeles enough to shake off the paparazzi. So she's trying something new—fighting back. The *Herbie: Fully Loaded* star is pressing charges against a photographer who she says rammed her Mercedes last month in pursuit of a shot. The accident spurred the Los Angeles police department to launch a probe into the increasingly aggressive tactics paparazzi employ to catch celebs in such newsworthy acts as picking up dry cleaning. Freeway shootings and gang violence are important, too, but someone's got to protect a starlet's right to park at the mall.

[Source: Rebecca Winters, *Time* magazine, June 12, 2005]

This was probably a very serious matter for actress and singer Lindsay Lohan. So, what do you make of the last sentence, which seems to suggest otherwise?

> *Through the telephoto lens*
> This long-range shot shows singer Mariah Carey on a yacht off the coast of Sardinia in the Mediterranean Sea. Was it right to photograph her without her knowledge?

Do we need stricter privacy laws?

Most celebrities agree that there need to be stricter privacy laws. But do you agree? Perhaps celebrities sometimes confuse the question of privacy with that of "**commercial confidentiality**." You might think that famous people sometimes guard their privacy because they know that they can release details about themselves, in an autobiography or an exclusive interview, for a lot of money.

Image rights

This issue is linked to celebrities' "image rights," which give them the exclusive right to control commercial use and exploitation of their image, voice, and likeness. Some celebrities try to get around the influence of the paparazzi. In May 2006 actress Angelina Jolie gave birth to a daughter, Shiloh. Knowing that paparazzi would try to photograph her baby, Jolie distributed images of Shiloh herself through a photographic agency. Magazines paid millions of dollars for the rights to publish the pictures, and the movie star donated the profits to charity.

When is a wedding "private"?

How "private" do you think a wedding is supposed to be? The wedding of movie stars Michael Douglas and Catherine Zeta-Jones resulted in a famous court case. Do you think the following report is unbiased? Do you think the writer meant it to be unbiased? Can you figure out the arguments that the Douglases would have used? Or the defense of *Hello!* magazine?

Zeta-Jones Result: Will Courts Create a Privacy Law?
Michael Douglas and Catherine Zeta-Jones won a High Court [British court] ruling on Friday that said *Hello!* magazine breached rights of commercial confidence by publishing photographs of the Hollywood golden couple's wedding; but the court found that there was no invasion of privacy. . . . . The wedding took place in November 2000. The couple sold the exclusive photo rights to the event to *OK!* magazine for $1.6 million, although they retained control over the selection of pictures that would appear in *OK!* A paparazzo intruder gained access to the wedding by bribing staff and surreptitiously took relatively poor photographs that were then bought for publication in *OK!*'s rival magazine, *Hello!* The Douglases and *OK!* initially obtained a court order to restrain publication; but the Court of Appeal acceded to *Hello!*'s arguments and lifted the **injunction**, leaving [the] Douglases to claim in damages [of $1.6 million]. *Hello!* published the unauthorized photographs on the same day as

OK!'s authorized coverage.

Justice Lindsay reasoned that the Douglases had a valuable trade asset, "a commodity the value of which depended, in part at least, upon its content at first being kept secret and then of its being made public in ways controlled by Miss Zeta-Jones and Mr. Douglas for the benefit of them and of [the publishers of OK!]."

[Source: OUT-LAW News, April, 14, 2003 (website of international law firm Pinsent Masons)]

> *Invasion of privacy or press freedom?*
Celebrity movie-star couple Catherine Zeta-Jones and Michael Douglas are snapped leaving the High Court in London in April 2003. The 2007 ruling overturning the appeal by *Hello!* magazine against the 2003 damages of $1.6 million is seen by some as a blow against the freedom of the press.

Extending press freedom

A country's free press can comment on the way in which society is run. The press loses all its power if it is not free to publish without interference. The following article defends the "new" press of **wikis**, weblogs (blogs), and specialized websites created by "citizen journalists."

```
EFF Fights to Unmuzzle Citizen Journalists
February 8, 2007, New York—The Electronic Frontier
Foundation (EFF) told a judge Wednesday to remove the legal
muzzle on citizen journalists caught up in a court battle
over documents relating to the controversial prescription
drug Zyprexa. EFF argues that the injunction against
publication of the documents online is prior restraint
on their free speech and a violation of First Amendment
rights. . . . In a brief filed with the court on Wednesday,
EFF explains that this is the digital equivalent of a "stop
the presses" order on individuals who were not involved in
the leak. The documents remain readily available on the
Internet from a variety of sources.

[Source: Electronic Frontier Foundation—http://eff.org/
legal/cases/zyprexa/brief_opposing_injunction.pdf
Available through http://creativecommons.org/licenses/
by/3.0]
```

First Amendment rights

This article mentions "First Amendment rights." The First Amendment to the U.S. Constitution states, among other things, "Congress shall make no law … abridging the freedom of speech, or of the press." Many see this as a fundamental freedom in the United States.

Thomas Jefferson, who became the third president of the United States, was one of the authors of the First Amendment. In a letter to a friend in 1787 he said, "Were it left to me to decide whether we should have a government without newspapers, or newspapers without a government, I should not hesitate a moment to prefer the latter."

Do you think that the First Amendment should never be violated? Or do you think there are special circumstances that override this right?

> *Parr is a one-man newspaper*
Barry Parr is one of a new breed of citizen journalists. He runs a popular online newspaper that covers local issues in his county in California. Are citizen journalists really members of the press, like those that work for traditional newspapers? What do you think?

 ## Citizen journalism

Did you notice the use of the phrase "citizen journalist" in the article on the opposite page? According to a report by the American Press Institute, **citizen journalism** involves ordinary people "playing an active role in the process of collecting, reporting, analyzing, and disseminating news and information." It includes things such as user comments on news stories, personal blogs, pictures captured by cell phones, and email newsletters. This kind of journalism is going to have more and more effect on privacy, too. On personal blogs, wikis, and other Internet sites, people are free to say what they like about others and are able to give details about them that those people might consider private.

Photos around the world

If you have a cell phone or your own camera, you have probably taken photos of your friends. What if you were encouraged to send some of the pictures to a website for some reason—perhaps for a competition? You might think this was fun, especially if the photos showed your friends in a funny light. But your friends (or their parents) might not be so pleased to see themselves on the Internet, available for all to see via the World Wide Web! That is where the question of invading someone else's privacy comes in. What if you were the photographed person? Would you think you had a right to privacy? Would that include not having your picture on the Internet without your knowledge or permission?

We're all celebrities!

We are all very desirable people to salesmen and saleswomen, especially if they think we could be interested in their product or service. The question of invasion of privacy comes in with the practice known as **telemarketing**. These calls are unsolicited—the person being called on the phone is not expecting the call. This is not always a very effective sales technique, but many companies accept that the vast majority of calls are a waste of time and yet continue with the practice. When you answer the phone, they may try to convince you that they are not selling anything but rather simply want to make you a special offer or ask you to take part in a short survey.

Do you think telemarketing is an invasion of privacy? Perhaps it would depend on what you were doing at the time, what time of day it was, or even what the product or service was. It might also depend on the attitude of the person making the call. You might feel sorry for that person, who is after all only doing his or her job and trying to earn a living.

What do they think?

"At my house telemarketers are never successful, so it does seem a waste of time and energy. They feel intrusive in the middle of, say, a family meal and the inevitable 'no, thank you' does become repetitive."
Bella, 18, student

"I'm in favor of any service that stops unsolicited calls. They are an invasion of my privacy and a complete waste of time. I don't object as strongly to junk mail if recycled paper is used."
Rosy, 45, freelance worker

> *India calling!*
>
> This busy call center is in Bangalore, India. Each person has a phone and computer terminal in his or her small cubicle.

Stopping the calls

Many countries have introduced laws to stop people from receiving telemarketing calls if they do not want to. In 2003 the U.S. Federal Trade Commission opened the "National Do Not Call Registry." The law says that telemarketers are not allowed to call registered numbers. They are required to search the registry at least once every 31 days and drop registered numbers from their call lists. Federal law also prohibits telemarketers from using automated diallers to call cell phones.

Do you agree that this registry is a reasonable service that helps protect people's privacy? Do you feel the same way about unsolicited mail and email, so-called junk mail? Or do you think that that is less intrusive, because you can at least open it when you want to?

> *George Orwell's vision of the future*
> These boys, shown in a movie version of George Orwell's *Nineteen Eighty-Four*, are so used to seeing images of their leader, Big Brother, that they barely notice.

Is Big Brother Watching You?

The famous phrase "Big Brother is watching you" comes from a novel by George Orwell that was published in 1949. The novel was called *Nineteen Eighty-Four*, the year in which the action takes place. This must have seemed like the distant future when the book came out, just after World War II (1939–45). The famous phrase referred to the leader of a political party that controls everyone's lives. This dictator, Big Brother, can see everything because all rooms have a "telescreen" that cannot be shut off. It both broadcasts the party's slogans and registers everything that happens in the room with the party's "Thought Police."

Since the publication of Orwell's book, the phrase "Big Brother" has been used to describe any invasive or controlling authority figure. The reality TV program *Big Brother* also takes its name from *Nineteen Eighty-Four*. In the show, contestants live in an isolated house and try to avoid being evicted by the public in order to win a cash prize. They are given instructions on what to do by a controlling character called Big Brother. Viewers can watch what they are doing all the time they are in the house. But is this really how we want our future reality to be?

Future possibilities

We might all agree that we would not want the future to be "Orwellian." This word is sometimes used to refer to a Big-Brother-like invasion of personal privacy by the state. But new technology already makes it possible for all of us to be watched much more than by a simple "telescreen." Some of this is being introduced in an attempt to reduce crime. Would you agree that using technology in this way is a good idea? What do you think about "event-data recorders" in people's cars? Read the following article and then see what you think.

Psst, Your Car Is Watching You

An electronic snoop may be recording your driving. Is it a boon to safety or an invasion of privacy?

It was nearly 11 on a balmy June night in Muttontown, a New York City suburb. Two teenagers raced fast cars down a tree-lined thoroughfare. . . . At an intersection, within a second of each other, both cars smashed into a red Jeep, killing a nurse and her fiancé. At the hospital, one of the youths told a detective they were driving 50 mph to 55 mph.

> *Touching the future*
> In the future we may use many more flat touch-screens and other high-tech devices for identification and other purposes.

But unbeknownst to the teens and their families, there was a hidden witness to the race. A palm-size microcomputer, embedded in the Corvette's air-bag system, revealed that the car was traveling 139 mph. The data, downloaded by police after the vehicle was impounded, convinced a grand jury to indict the youths on murder charges, based on "depraved indifference to human life." In the end, they pleaded guilty to manslaughter and assault, and are now serving a three-year prison term. . . . A debate is surging over the black boxes technically called event-data recorders (EDRs). While some welcome them as a safety measure, others fear them as an Orwellian intrusion. . . . Privacy activists want the government to prevent police and insurance companies from checking drivers' black boxes without permission.

[Source: Margot Roosevelt, *Time* magazine, August 7, 2006]

How far?

Another fast-growing area is crime-detection by identifying **DNA**. This is the natural material in all of us that carries genetic information. DNA found at a crime scene can help the police identify a criminal, because everyone's DNA profile is unique. Because of this, the police may require suspects or others to supply DNA. This could be made compulsory for the whole population. But would this be a good idea? How far do you think we should go with these new developments? Should we be prepared to give up some of our privacy in order to help reduce crime?

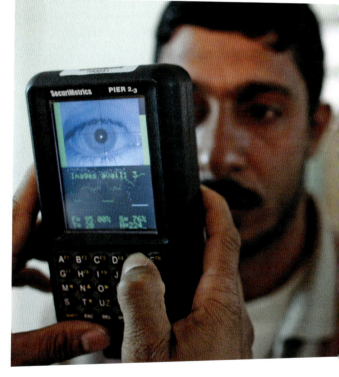

> *Futuristic security*

An Iraqi citizen has a scan of his retina (the back of his eye) taken for identification purposes by a U.S. Marine.

Summary

The central question of this book is: "Do we have a right to privacy?" After all you have read, you should be able to give your own informed answer to that question. As part of that answer, you will need to question your own opinions about privacy.

To make an overall decision about whether we have a right to privacy, you will need to make a decision on each of the different issues in this book. Then, you could give each of them a level of significance. An issue can be significant in two different ways. It can have what is called quantitative significance, which means that it affects a lot of people. It can also have qualitative significance, meaning that it affects people in a serious way. The use of security cameras affects a lot of people, so it has a lot of quantitative significance. But the effect it has might be small—you might only know about it if you commit a crime—so it might not have a lot of qualitative significance. On the other hand, the invasion of a celebrity's privacy undoubtedly has a lot of qualitative significance for the person involved, but the total number of people affected is relatively small, so the quantitative significance is lower.

Issues to think about

Many different aspects of privacy are covered in this book. Here is a list of some of the questions raised by the different issues. They are presented in the order in which they appear in the book:

- Is privacy a basic human right?
- Is databank technology leading to an invasion of people's privacy?
- Does the wish to defend people against acts of terrorism justify reducing their right to privacy?
- Does the USA PATRIOT Act undermine the civil liberties of Americans?
- Do identity cards represent an infringement of people's privacy?
- Should ID cards be compulsory?
- Is it right or wrong to keep a central databank of people's medical records?
- How much Internet privacy should people be allowed?
- Are websites' privacy policies good enough?
- Should email be made more secure?
- Should an employer be able to check all his or her employees' emails and website visits?
- Are there too many or too few CCTV cameras on our streets?
- Does the wish to reduce crime justify reducing everyone's privacy?
- Does freedom of the press justify investigating people's private lives?

- Are pictures of celebrities always in the public interest?
- Does it make any difference whether a photographer is working in a public or a private place?
- Do we need a general privacy law?
- Will "citizen journalism" lead to a loss of privacy for some people?
- Is telemarketing an invasion of privacy?

> *Staying informed*

Newspapers are a good way to gain up-to-date information. Some can be accessed online. But be careful, because journalists also present their own personal views on issues, so you have to sort fact from opinion.

Organizing your own debate

A debate is a formal discussion of a topic. It is a good way to examine issues on that topic, which may be in the form of a question—in our case, "Do we have a right to privacy?" Or the topic might be covered by a **proposition** (statement)—"We all have a right to privacy." People involved in the debate may argue in favor of the proposition or against it. In some formats, they may take another position entirely, reaching a conclusion that "maybe" or "in some cases" is better than "yes" or "no."

How to debate

There are many different ways to organize a debate. A few different formats are listed here. Make sure, when you debate, that you make complete arguments. Be careful to refute your opponent's arguments—that is, show how and why they are wrong. Each of these formats has a set of rules, which you can alter according to the number of participants and the amount of time you have available for the debate.

Two-sided debate

One side makes a case *for* the proposition. The other side argues *against* it. The side arguing for the proposition is called the affirmative. The other side is called the **opposition** or the negative. The first speaker on each side makes a speech. The sides alternate speakers. The affirmative team, which must try to show that the proposition is more likely to be true, speaks first and last. The opening affirmative speaker makes a case. The first opposition speaker refutes the case. Second speakers continue with their team's points and refute new points from the other side. The final speeches are summaries of the best arguments for a team and the best refutation against the major points of the other side.

With six students, you could have the following format and speaker times:

1st speaker, affirmative—5 minutes

1st speaker, opposition—5 minutes

2nd speaker, affirmative—5 minutes

2nd speaker, opposition—5 minutes

3rd speaker, opposition—3 minutes

3rd speaker, affirmative—3 minutes

You could add question-and-answer time by the class or audience during, in between, or after speeches.

Panel discussion

A group of students can participate in a roundtable discussion on an issue. Students speak for themselves and may agree or disagree with the opinions of others on the panel. The discussion is designed to inform an audience. There should be an overall time limit—for example, 30 minutes—for the entire discussion. You can use a **moderator** to ask questions and keep the discussion moving. A panel discussion is an opportunity to use conversation in a way that presents and challenges ideas. Audience questions may be added after the discussion.

> *Debating skills*
These students in New York are taking part in a debate. They have prepared notes to help them remember the points they want to make.

Open forum

An open forum is an effective format for a class or large group. A single moderator leads an open discussion on a range of topics related to an issue. Members of the audience may present new ideas, add to the presentations from others, or refute any argument. Like brainstorming (group discussions used to produce ideas), this format quickly gets a variety of ideas into a discussion. You could allow an individual or a small panel to judge a debate, voting on the outcome. For larger discussions, you could ask an audience which speaker did best and why.

All opinions count

For many of the issues covered in this book, you have read two or more varying points of view. It is important to remember that in order to reach an informed, balanced, unbiased view, you must take all these opinions into account. Do not dismiss right away those opinions you disagree with. Instead, ask yourself why you disagree with those opinions and present a good argument against them. You are then in a much stronger position to convince others of your considered views. So, what do you think? Do we have a right to privacy?

Find Out More

Projects

Websites' privacy policies

If you look at any major website, you will find small print at the bottom of the home page that includes the words "Privacy policy" (see page 24). Check a few of these out and see if and how they differ. The policy should tell you how that organization or company uses any information it may gain about you. Do some sites tell you more than others? Are you satisfied with these policies, and do they give you all the information you want?

Identity theft

You could look further at the issue of identity theft (see page 21). How do criminals get private information about people? How can people protect themselves? Do you think tighter privacy laws would help prevent identity theft?

Conduct your own survey

You could conduct your own survey on some of the issues raised in this book. Look again at the opinion poll quoted on page 18. Which topics would you like to get people's views on? You could try identity cards or CCTV. Write clear questions that your subjects can answer easily. Remember, however, that these will not necessarily be informed opinions that you are gathering—they may well be based on very little information.

Forecasting the future

What do you think the future holds for privacy rights and privacy laws? How much will they be affected by new technology? You can find out more by putting keywords, such as "biometrics," into an Internet search engine.

Websites

www.pueblo.gsa.gov/privacy_resources.htm
The U.S. Federal Citizen Information Center gives links to a list of "privacy resources" in the United States.

www.privacyinternational.org/index.shtml
Privacy International is a human rights group that works as a watchdog on surveillance and privacy invasion (see page 20); it has conducted campaigns on issues ranging from wiretapping and national security to ID cards, video surveillance, and freedom of information and expression. The website gives a great deal of well-argued information *for* the proposition that we all have a right to privacy.

www.un.org/Overview/rights.html
The United Nations' full text of the Universal Declaration of Human Rights (see page 11) is presented here. It is surprisingly easy to read and a good introduction to the whole issue of human rights from a legal and philosophical point of view.

Glossary

acronym   word formed from the initials or other letters in a name or phrase. For example, the acronym "NASA" is used to stand for the National Aeronautics and Space Administration.

advocate   supporter; person who speaks in favor of something

biased   showing unfair preference for or against something or someone; prejudiced

biometrics   measurement and scanning of physical characteristics (such as fingerprints, faces, or eyes) to verify a person's identity

CCTV   closed-circuit television, a surveillance system in which cameras transmit pictures by cables to monitors

censorship   not allowing certain books to be published or movies to be shown, or cutting out parts of them

citizen   person who has a legal right to live in a particular country

citizen journalism   also known as participatory journalism. It is ordinary citizens collecting and reporting news and other information. It can be published or broadcast in traditional formats, such as paper newsletters, or using online distribution.

civil liberties   basic rights of citizens guaranteed by law, such as freedom of speech

commercial confidentiality   secrecy surrounding business affairs, so that they are not revealed to competitors or the public

DNA   deoxyribonucleic acid, a substance in humans and other living things that carries genetic information

human rights   rights that most people believe apply to everyone, including basic freedoms

identity theft   use of another person's name and personal information, such as bank details, to steal from him or her

imperative   absolutely necessary, essential

injunction	court order that requires someone to do something or (very often) not to do something
judicial review	examination by a high court (for example, the Supreme Court) into whether a law introduced by the government is valid
moderator	chairperson of a debate, who guides it without taking sides
non-citizen	person who is not a citizen of a particular country
opposition	people in a debate who speak against the proposition
paparazzi	photographers who specialize in pursuing celebrities to get pictures of them
proposition	statement that expresses an opinion or a judgment
telemarketing	telephoning people unexpectedly to try to sell them goods or services
United Nations	international organization formed in 1945 to promote world peace, security, and cooperation among nations
wiki	piece of server software that lets users collaborate—meaning they are all able to add or edit content—on a webpage
wiretapping	connecting secretly to someone's telephone line or email address to listen to or read his or her messages

Index

Amnesty International 17–18
arguments 6, 50
  assertions 6
  evidence 6, 7
  reasoning 6, 7
  refutation 50
  see also debate
  assumptions 6, 7

bias 6, 7, 19, 38
Big Brother 44, 45, 46
biometrics 32–33
brainstorming 51

camera surveillance 16, 29–33, 48
Carey, Mariah 37
celebrities 8, 34, 35, 36–39, 48, 49
censorship 35
civil liberties 18, 19
closed-circuit television (CCTV) 29, 30–31, 32, 48
commercial confidentiality 38
cookies 26
crime 13, 20, 21, 22, 30, 46–47, 48
critical thinking 6, 7

databanks 12, 13, 14–15, 16, 23, 32, 48
debate 49–51
  moderator 50, 51
  open forum 51
  roundtable discussion 50
  two-sided debate 50
DNA 47
Douglas, Michael 38–39

educational records 18
email encryption 26
  junk mail 43

monitoring 18, 26, 27, 48
emotive language 19
European Convention on Human Rights 11
event-data recorders 46–47

face-recognition devices 32, 33
facts 6, 7, 35
financial records 18

hackers 13, 26
human rights 10, 11, 17, 18, 48

identity cards 13, 20–21, 48
identity theft 13, 21, 22
image rights 38
Internet email 18, 26, 27, 43, 48
online newspapers 40, 41
posting photos on 42
privacy 23-7, 48
privacy policies 24
issues 5
qualitative significance 48
quantitative significance 48

Jolie, Angelina 38
journalism
  citizen journalism 40, 41, 49
  First Amendment 40
  invasive journalism 35
  press freedom 33, 35, 40, 48
junk mail 42, 43

logic, sound 6
Lohan, Lindsay 37
London Underground bombings (2005) 30

medical records 16, 22, 23, 48

Nineteen Eighty-Four (Orwell) 44, 45

online newspapers 40, 41

opinions 5, 35
  informed opinions 5, 6

paparazzi 36, 37, 38
  see also camera surveillance
personal identification numbers (PINs) 33
photographing
  celebrities 8, 34, 35, 36–39, 49
  on the Internet 42

privacy rights 5, 9, 10, 11, 16, 36, 48
public interest 35

rights
  human rights 10, 11, 17, 18, 48
  see also privacy rights

September 11, 2001, terrorist attacks 16, 18, 29
smart systems 32

telemarketing 42–43, 49
terrorism 16, 17, 19, 29, 30, 48

United Nations 10, 11
Universal Declaration of Human Rights 11, 16
USA PATRIOT Act 16–19, 48

verification devices 13, 33
views, comparing and contrasting 19

"war on terror" 16, 18, 19
weblogs (blogs) 40, 41
wikis 40, 41
wiretapping 16, 18

Zeta-Jones, Catherine 38–39